77

CHIEF SEATTLE
GREAT STATESMAN

BY ELIZABETH RIDER MONTGOMERY

ILLUSTRATED BY RUSS HOOVER

GARRARD PUBLISHING COMPANY
CHAMPAIGN, ILLINOIS

ALICE MARRIOTT and CAROL K. RACHLIN of Southwest Research Associates are consultants for Garrard Indian Books.

MISS MARRIOTT has lived among the Kiowa and Cheyenne Indians in Oklahoma and spent many years with the Pueblos of New Mexico and the Hopis of Arizona. First woman to take a degree in anthropology from the University of Oklahoma, she is a Fellow of the American Anthropological Association, now working with its Curriculum Project.

MISS RACHLIN, also a Fellow of AAA and of the American Association for the Advancement of Science, is a graduate in anthropology of Columbia University. She has done archaeological work in New Jersey and Indiana, and ethnological field work with Algonquian tribes of the Midwest.

Contents

Suquamish Indians

Chief Seattle's people, the Suquamish, were one of the peaceable Puget Sound Area tribes. They were part of the larger group of wealthy Pacific Northwest Coast Indians.

These Indians lived in large wooden houses along rivers and on bays. Food was plentiful. In the spring and summer they went fishing and gathered enough berries and roots for the winter. During the long, mild winters, they planned elaborate ceremonies, carved fishing canoes and other objects, and wove blankets.

Winter was the time for families to give great feasts called potlatches. Guests were entertained by singing and dancing and were given many gifts. The most important family was the one giving the most gifts to its guests.

Northwest Coast Indians were known for their wealth, their ceremonies and handcrafts, and especially their potlatches.

1. Restoration Point, where Vancouver landed and See-at-hl saw his first white men.

2. Ole-man-house, where war councils and victory celebrations were held.

3. Alki Point, where the first "Bostons" settled.

4. The Duwamish River, where Chief Seattle's men helped the settlers find wapatoes.

5. Seattle, named in honor of the chief who wanted peace.

6. The White River valley, where the Muckleshoots killed many settlers.

1

The "Bird Canoe"

Little See-at-hl was as excited as all the rest of the Suquamish Indians. The whole tribe ran up and down the beach. Everybody shouted and pointed at the ship sailing toward them. They thought its sails were wings.

"What can it be?"

"It's an enormous bird!"

"No, it's a great canoe! It's a bird canoe!"

Suddenly smoke rose from the ship. "BOOM!"

The Indians ran into the woods. The boy See-at-hl ran too. Surely something dreadful was about to happen!

It was May 19, 1792, on the shore of what is now Bainbridge Island in Puget Sound. The "bird canoe" was Captain Vancouver's ship. Captain Vancouver was a great English explorer, the first white man to sail into the northwest corner of the United States.

Vancouver thought he had never seen such beautiful green country. For three weeks he had been exploring a long arm of the Pacific Ocean. He named it Puget Sound. The shores of the sound were lined with tall evergreen trees. Behind were snow-capped mountains.

8

The Indians watched as the "bird canoe" stopped moving and folded its wings. Darkness fell. See-at-hl wondered if the ship would fly away in the night.

When morning came, the ship was still there. A small boat was lowered. Strange men came to the island.

See-at-hl pressed close to his father, Chief Schweabe. "They all paint themselves with light paint!" he whispered.

"That is not paint," Chief Schweabe whispered back. "They are white men. Our medicine men foretold that white men would come to our shores."

Exactly 300 years earlier, in 1492, Columbus had come to the eastern shores of America. Since then, stories of white men had traveled west, from one Indian tribe to another.

The Suquamish chiefs went to meet Captain Vancouver. They talked to him with gestures. He gave them gifts.

The next day some Indians visited Vancouver's ship. See-at-hl went with them. They paddled in a big circle around the "bird canoe." They sang their canoe song. Vancouver's crew helped the visitors aboard.

On the ship, the little Indian boy saw many wonderful things. He saw sharp knives made of iron. He saw forks used for eating. He saw cooking kettles made from metal instead of reeds. He saw fire-sticks called guns.

Captain Vancouver was kind. He gave See-at-hl bread and molasses. The little boy liked these strange foods.

"White men are good," he said to his father as they left the ship. "I like white men."

A week later the ship sailed away. See-at-hl watched the "bird canoe" out of sight. He hoped he would see white men again.

2

Guardian Spirit

All that summer See-at-hl's people camped on one beach after another to fish. They dried many salmon to eat that winter. Fish was the main food of the Suquamish Indians.

Every day See-at-hl bathed in a stream. He swam in the sound. He learned to shoot with a bow and arrow. He learned how a fish trap was built and how salmon nets and spears were used.

Only men and boys fished for salmon. The women dried the salmon which the men caught. They dug clams and roots and picked berries.

When the winter rains began, See-at-hl and his people went back to their winter home. This was a long house by the sound. It was made of cedar planks.

All winter See-at-hl lived in the long house with his father and mother. Each family in the tribe had its own part of an apartment.

See-at-hl played in the soft rain with his friends. He watched men as they made canoes and carved doorposts. He watched women weaving blankets and baskets. He bathed daily in a creek. There was seldom any snow on Puget Sound.

See-at-hl enjoyed the long winter evenings. Then people gathered in the potlatch house, which was for feasts and parties. See-at-hl sat by the fire with the men and boys. He enjoyed the medicine men's dances and their stories of white men.

The happy summers and winters passed quickly. When See-at-hl was twelve years old, his father said, "Now you must find your guardian spirit, my son. It will help you all your life."

See-at-hl's father gave him a burning torch. His mother gave him a cedar-bark belt. See-at-hl put on the belt and went out in the winter rain alone to find his guardian spirit.

He walked for miles. At last he came to another beach.

See-at-hl built a fire. He bathed in a stream. Then he walked and walked in the green forest. But he did not find a spirit.

See-at-hl came back to the beach and swam in the cold water. But he did not find a spirit there. When night came, he slept by his fire without a blanket.

The next morning See-at-hl was hungry. How he wished he had a necklace of dried clams! But he must eat nothing until he found a spirit. He tightened his belt. He bathed, and then he started out again.

Day after day See-at-hl walked and swam. After a few days he was no longer hungry. But his head felt very light. Sometimes he was not sure whether he was asleep or awake.

One day See-at-hl sat on a big log and paddled far out on the sound. Then he dove down into the deep water. Down, down, down he went. His lungs felt as though they were on fire. He kicked and struggled to reach the air again. Then the world around him turned black.

The next thing See-at-hl knew he was lying on the beach. The rain beat on his face. The waves of the sound washed over his feet. He opened his eyes. A white seagull flew over him.

See-at-hl knew this was not an ordinary bird. It was his guardian spirit. Never as long as he lived would See-at-hl kill a seagull.

3

The Potlatch

When See-at-hl returned home, Chief Schweabe said, "Now you are a man. We will celebrate with a potlatch." This was a special kind of party.

Schweabe invited the Duwamish and other friendly tribes. The Suquamish Indians began to get ready. The men killed deer, elk and ducks. The women dug clams. Everybody worked for days.

By the time the first canoes arrived,
meat was cooking over the open fires.
Clams steamed over hot stones. Roots
boiled in watertight baskets.

As each canoe approached, the visitors
sang their family songs. The Suquamish
Indians sang their songs in reply. The
women did a dance of greeting. The
children danced too.

Schweabe and See-at-hl, dressed in
their finest clothes, welcomed the guests.
They led them into the potlatch house.
Food was served in great carved bowls
and on plates.

After dinner some of the guests made
speeches. Then See-at-hl made one too.
People were surprised that a boy could
make such a fine speech.

"See-at-hl will be a good leader," the old men said to each other.

For days there was eating and speechmaking, and singing and dancing. There were many games, too.

The last day of the party was the time for the potlatch, or gift-giving. Chief Schweabe had a big pile of gifts ready. He gave his guests blankets, canoes, paddles, baskets, mats, nets, ornaments, bows, arrows, spears and shell money. He gave away nearly everything he had.

"Schweabe is a very great chief," the guests said. "This was a fine potlatch."

The visitors loaded the gifts in their canoes and started home. Some day they too would give potlatches. They would invite Chief Schweabe and

See-at-hl. They would try to give more gifts than they had received today.

See-at-hl watched the canoes leave. He remembered proudly what the old men had said.

"Some day I shall be a great chief like my father," he thought.

4

War Chief

A scout brought dreadful news to the Suquamish village.

"The river tribes are coming!"

See-at-hl was now 21. He knew what the warning meant. Their enemies, the Muckleshoots, were on the warpath. They would attack the peaceful Puget Sound Indians. Men would be killed. Women and children would be made slaves.

Chief Schweabe called six tribes to a war council in Ole-man-house. This was a big apartment house by the sound, with about 40 apartments. Sometimes 700 people lived there. Ole-man-house was 1,000 feet long. Posts seven feet thick held up the roof. Pictures were carved and painted on them.

As usual the oldest men spoke first.

"We must hide," said old Chief Kitsap. "Only in the forest will we be safe."

"No," said Schweabe. "The Suquamish will be safer here in Ole-man-house. I will bring them all inside."

One after another the old men spoke. Not one of them had a plan for everybody. These tribes had never before worked together.

At last it was the turn of the young men to speak. See-at-hl was the first. His voice was deep and powerful. All the Indians listened.

"If we must fight," said See-at-hl, "let us all fight together. One tribe is weak, but six tribes will be strong." He told them his plan to trap the enemy.

"See-at-hl has spoken well," said the young Indians.

"It is a wise plan," the old men agreed. The Indians elected See-at-hl war chief to lead the six Puget Sound tribes.

When his warriors were ready, Chief See-at-hl led them up the White River to a bend in the stream. There were high banks on each side.

"We will set a trap here," See-at-hl told them.

The Indians cut down a great fir tree with stone tools. It took many hours. At last the tree fell across the river, stretching from one bank to the other. It could not be seen above the bend.

Then See-at-hl and his warriors hid. It was not long before five big canoes came down the river. Each one was filled with Indians in bright war paint.

Quick as an arrow, the first canoe came around the bend. The current was very swift. Too late the Indians saw the big tree. They could not go around it. They could not go under it. The canoe smashed into the tree and upset. The Indians fell into the water.

See-at-hl and his men rushed out of the woods. Not a single enemy reached the shore.

Another canoe came down the river, and then another. The same thing happened each time.

Then the last two canoes came. This time the river Indians could tell that something was wrong. Instead of going around the bend they headed for the shore. Chief See-at-hl and his warriors captured them.

5

Peacetime Chief

The Puget Sound tribes met at Ole-man-house to celebrate their victory. A young Duwamish made up a song about the battle. He acted it out in a dance. Other young warriors joined in.

When the dance ended, the young Indians cried, "See-at-hl is a great war chief!"

Then See-at-hl made a speech. "We won the battle because we all fought together," he said. "Now let us all join together as one great tribe. Then other Indians will fear to make war on us. We can have peace forever."

The Indians agreed, and See-at-hl was elected head chief of the Six Allied Tribes: the Duwamish, the Suquamish, the Samahmish and three small tribes. The chief of each tribe became a sub-chief under See-at-hl. All the chiefs lived at Ole-man-house.

For a while everything went well. Then some of the tribes wanted to break away from the Allied Tribes. Chief See-at-hl did not want this to happen. He visited the tribes with his warriors. He talked to the chiefs.

"If you leave the Allied Tribes you will be small and weak," See-at-hl told them. "Enemies will attack you. Stay with us, and my warriors will protect you."

The Indians listened to See-at-hl. They looked at his brave young warriors. They decided to stay with the Allied Tribes.

Many years passed. They were years of peace for the Puget Sound Indians. See-at-hl was a wise leader. He made treaties of friendship with other tribes. He gave grand potlatches. His people were happy.

See-at-hl married and had a daughter named Kick-es-om-la. When his wife died, he married again and had five more sons and daughters.

After Vancouver's visit, See-at-hl had seen no white men for several years. Then a sailing ship from Boston came to the Pacific Coast. After that the Indians called Americans "Bostons" or "Postons."

See-at-hl did not like Boston ships. White sailors taught the Indians to lie and steal. They traded them firewater which made them a little crazy.

In 1806 See-at-hl heard about the explorers Lewis and Clark. They came overland to the Pacific Coast. After Lewis and Clark, many white men came west. Some were trappers who killed beaver and mink. Some were store-keepers like the Hudson's Bay Company men. And some were "Black Robes," priests who taught Indians about God.

Chief See-at-hl learned about the white man's God. He tried to get his people to follow the teachings of the priests.

Many settlers came to the west coast. They built the towns of San Francisco and Portland, far to the south of Oleman-house. They built Olympia which was much nearer. It was at the end of Puget Sound, only four sleeps away.

Then when See-at-hl was about 60, settlers came to his own land.

6

The Coming of the Bostons

It was the end of summer in 1851. Chief See-at-hl's people were fishing for salmon near Alki Point. This was across the sound from Bainbridge Island.

A small boat arrived. Three young "Bostons" got out. Their names were David Denny, John Low and Lee Terry. Using signs, they told See-at-hl they wanted a canoe and a guide. They were looking for a place to build homes.

They had crossed the mountains in covered wagons. Their families were in Portland, and would soon come to Puget Sound.

See-at-hl had long known that settlers would come to his land one day. Some western tribes had had trouble with the whites. But See-at-hl decided to make friends with them. He let the young men have two guides and a canoe.

After they looked around, the Bostons decided to build their homes at Alki Point. They started to cut down trees for a cabin.

Soon Low and Terry left, and David Denny was alone.

See-at-hl watched the young Boston with interest. David kept working on the cabin. He cut his foot on an axe.

He fell sick with a fever. But he did not give up. See-at-hl was pleased. This was a brave young white chief.

On November 13, a "bird canoe" laid anchor off Alki Point. See-at-hl watched as a small boat was lowered. The boat came to the shore. Many white people got out. Half of them were children. One was a tiny baby.

It was raining hard. The white women and children tried to get out of the rain. The cabin had no roof so they sat on logs under the trees.

The white men rowed to the ship. They brought boxes, barrels and tools to the beach. Then the ship left.

Soon David Denny brought the other settlers to meet Chief See-at-hl. "This is my brother Arthur," he said.

See-at-hl shook hands with Arthur Denny, Carson Boren, Charles Terry and William Bell. "Welcome to the green land," he said. "We will live together as brothers."

The settlers did not understand the words, but they knew See-at-hl was friendly. They thanked him.

That winter Chief See-at-hl and his people did not live at Ole-man-house. The Suquamish and Duwamish Indians camped at Alki Point.

The Indians taught the Bostons to fish for salmon and dig clams. When the baby had no milk, they taught his mother to feed him on clam juice.

The settlers finished two log cabins. They wanted to build another. But there were no more small trees nearby for log walls.

Chief See-at-hl pointed to some huge cedar trees. "Big trees will make good lodges," he told the settlers.

Arthur Denny shook his head. "We need smaller logs for cabin walls," he said.

"My people will show you what to do," said the chief.

The Indians cut down a great cedar tree. They stripped off the bark to use for rope, baskets and clothes. Then using a sharp stone they split the big log into slabs. The cedar split cleanly and evenly.

"Cabin walls," said Chief See-at-hl.

After that the settlers built slab houses instead of log cabins.

The Indians liked the settlers, but they could not understand their ways. White women wanted the Indians to knock before coming into their cabins. They became angry when Indians helped themselves to food.

"Bostons do not share as Indians do," See-at-hl told his people. "We must learn white man's ways. Then we can live together in peace."

7

The City of Seattle

Chief See-at-hl sat in his big canoe. He looked at the handsome white doctor he was taking to Alki. He was pleased.

It was March, 1852. Chief See-at-hl had gone to Olympia and persuaded Dr. David Maynard to come with him.

"The new settlement needs a doctor," the chief said. "There has been much sickness." See-at-hl's own wife had died during the winter.

Dr. Maynard smiled. "I don't believe there will be enough sickness to keep me busy, Chief," he said. "But I can do other things besides doctoring."

It took four days to reach Alki Point. Most of the settlers had moved across the bay to a good harbor. See-at-hl took the doctor to meet them.

The Bostons had built a new settlement there. A man named Henry Yesler put up a steam sawmill. It ran day and night. Indians as well as Bostons worked there. They cut down trees and shipped big logs to San Francisco.

Dr. Maynard helped the settlement to grow. He built a store. He bought salmon from the Indians. He salted salmon and shipped it to San Francisco.

He hired Indians to cut down trees on his land. New settlers arrived. Dr. Maynard sold land to them. He took care of the sick—white or Indian.

Chief See-at-hl and Dr. Maynard became good friends. The doctor learned to speak Indian languages. The Indians trusted him. They came to see him when they were sick or in trouble.

Many Indians camped near Dr. Maynard's store. Among them were See-at-hl and his grownup daughter Kick-es-om-la. The Bostons called her Angeline.

Angeline became friends with Dr. Maynard's new wife. The doctor had brought her from Olympia. Catherine Maynard was a good, kind woman. She helped her husband care for the sick.

January, 1853, was very cold. Snow fell. The settlers ran out of flour and potatoes. They could not get any more until a ship came from San Francisco.

"My people will help you," said See-at-hl. He sent four Indians up the Duwamish River with Arthur Denny and John Low. They got 50 bushels of wapatoes, a kind of wild potato.

"Chief See-at-hl is a good friend," said the settlers.

In May, 1853, the Bostons decided to name their town.

"This will be a big city some day," said William Bell. "We should call it London or Paris."

"No," said Arthur Denny. "Our town should have a special name."

Dr. Maynard spoke up. "Chief See-at-hl has been a good friend. Let us name our town after him."

"See-at-hl is much too hard to say," objected Carson Boren.

"Only an Indian can say that name right," Henry Yesler agreed.

The doctor thought a moment. Then he said, "We'll change it a little. 'Seattle' is easy to say."

Everybody liked that. So the settlers named their little town "Seattle." Dr. Maynard told the chief about it.

"No! No!" cried See-at-hl. "My name must not be spoken after I am dead! Every time my name is repeated, my spirit will turn over!"

"Do not worry, Chief," the doctor answered. "When people say 'Seattle' they will be speaking of a city, not of you. Your spirit will rest in peace."

See-at-hl trusted Dr. Maynard. He did not worry any more about the town's name.

Soon the chief was known as "Seattle" too. In time he became very proud that the city had been named for him.

8

Chief Seattle Speaks

Chief Seattle and his son were among a crowd of Indians sitting on the beach by Dr. Maynard's store. They had come to meet the new governor.

It was late December, 1853. So many Bostons had come to the northwest that the Washington Territory had been formed. President Pierce had sent Isaac Stevens to govern it.

Dr. Maynard introduced Governor Stevens, and the Little White Chief began to speak. He talked very fast. His words were like hail beating against Chief Seattle's ears.

"The Great White Chief in the city of Washington loves the Indians," said Governor Stevens. "He wishes to care for you, to teach you, to protect you. He will move you to a place of your own, called a reservation."

The governor said a reservation would be a kingdom, but Seattle knew it would really be a prison. Indians were used to wandering wherever they wished.

Suquamish and Duwamish Indians had always lived in the west, but other tribes had been pushed westward by the whites for 300 years. Now Indians could go no farther west, for the ocean was in the way.

Governor Stevens said the Indians would be paid for their land. There would be a treaty. But the Indians believed that land belonged to everybody, like air and water. How could land be sold?

The Indians looked at Chief Seattle. They wanted him to speak for them. Slowly he got up. Tall and stately, he stood beside the little governor. In his trumpet-like voice he began to speak.

"The Great White Chief wishes to buy our lands," Seattle said. "This appears just, even generous. He says that if we do as he desires he will protect us. Then he will be our father and we his children.

"But can that ever be? Your God is not our God. Your God makes your people strong. Soon they will fill the land. Our people are ebbing away like a tide that will never return. The White Man's God cannot love our people or he would protect them."

Chief Seattle had dreamed of Indians and Bostons sharing the green land. But that was not to be. The Great White Chief wanted the Indians penned up in reservations. The Indians would either have to go there or fight.

Many Indians wanted to fight. A young Nisqually Chief, Leschi, was one of these. But Chief Seattle knew that Indians had never won a war against the whites. It was better to go to a reservation than to fight a hopeless war.

"Day and night cannot dwell together," said Chief Seattle sadly. "It seems that my people must retire to the reservation you offer them. Then we will dwell apart in peace.

"It matters little where we pass the remnant of our days. They will not be many. A few more moons, a few more winters, and not one red man will remain."

Seattle looked around at the white settlers. He said:

"When the last red man shall have perished . . . these shores will swarm with the invisible dead of my tribe. When your children's children think themselves alone in the field, the store, the shop, upon the highway, or in the silence of the pathless woods, they will

not be alone. . . . At night when the streets of your city are silent, and you think them deserted, they will throng with the returning hosts that . . . still love this beautiful land. The white man will never be alone."

Chief Seattle looked down at the little governor. His voice became stern.

"Let him be just and deal kindly with my people, for the dead are not powerless. Dead, did I say? There is no death, only a change of worlds."

9

Treaty Troubles

A year later Governor Stevens returned to Puget Sound for the treaty-signing. Chief Seattle and his son walked along the shore to the meeting.

Dr. Maynard had tried to persuade Governor Stevens to change his plans for the Indians. But the governor would not listen. All year long Stevens rushed from one Indian council to another. He talked to hundreds of Indian tribes in Washington, in Idaho and in Montana.

He planned reservations and treaties and did not ask what the Indians wanted.

"I know Indians better than anyone else ever has!" he boasted.

Chief Seattle remembered the treaty Stevens had offered Leschi's tribe. The Nisquallies were farming Indians. But they could never farm on the reservation Governor Stevens gave them. Leschi had become very angry.

"That reservation is nothing but worthless gravel which the Bostons do not want!" the handsome young chief cried. "My people would starve there!" Leschi would not sign the treaty.

Now it was time for Chief Seattle's people to sign their treaty. Seattle listened carefully as the treaty was explained.

The reservation would be 1280 acres around Ole-man-house. That was good, Chief Seattle thought. The Indians could fish and dig clams as they had always done.

Dr. Maynard would be the Indian agent. He would live on the reservation, and take care of the Indians when they were sick. He would help them get used to reservation life. That was good. All the Indians liked Dr. Maynard and his wife.

The Muckleshoots would live on the reservation with the Puget Sound Indians. That was bad. The Muckleshoots had always been their enemies.

"There will be trouble about this reservation," Chief Seattle told Dr. Maynard.

"It is foolish to put enemies together on the same reservation," the doctor agreed. "I will talk to the governor."

The stubborn little governor would not listen to Dr. Maynard. "Put your mark on the treaty now," he told Seattle and the other chiefs.

Chief Seattle rose. He did not like the treaty, but he believed there would be war if the Indians did not sign it. No good could come from war.

"My people will do as the Great White Father in Washington City asks," said Seattle. "Our tribes will keep their word. Let the White Chief keep his word too. Let there be peace between us." Seattle made his mark on the treaty as chief of the Duwamish and Suquamish.

The governor gave the Indians cheap gifts: straw hats, Jews' harps, and some molasses. Then he rushed off to another treaty meeting.

Soon there was terrible trouble. The Muckleshoots did not want to live with the Puget Sound Indians. They were very angry about the treaty. They blamed the white settlers for it. They killed all of the people who had settled in the White River valley.

Leschi refused to go to the Nisqually reservation. Governor Stevens sent soldiers to arrest him. They did not find Leschi, but fighting broke out between the soldiers and the Indians.

All over Washington Territory there was trouble between Indians and whites. President Pierce sent a warship, the *Decatur*, to guard the town of Seattle.

"War is surely coming," Chief Seattle told Dr. Maynard. "My people want to join Leschi and fight the Bostons."

"We must move your people to the reservation," said the doctor. "It will be easier to keep them peaceful there."

Governor Stevens had promised that the government would send the Indians money. But no money came. So Dr. Maynard bought them food and blankets with his own money. He bought lumber for lodges too. In November, 1855, the doctor helped Chief Seattle and his people move to the reservation.

A few weeks later a visitor came to a council meeting at Ole-man-house. It was Leschi.

"I have risked my life to come here," Leschi said. "Soldiers are after me."

"Why did you come?" asked Seattle.

"I came to ask you to join your Indian brothers," the Nisqually chief answered. "We will kill all the Bostons. Then the good Mother Earth will be ours again."

Many Indians wanted to join Leschi. But Seattle refused.

"Wars settle nothing," Seattle said. "Besides, Indians can never win against the Bostons."

"This war will be different," Leschi answered. "We have guns now, not just bows and arrows."

"I cannot go to war," Seattle said. "I have given my word."

"Why should you keep your word?" asked Leschi. "The Bostons break their word to you."

It was true. The money the governor promised had not come. No gifts had come. The treaty paper had not been sent.

Still Seattle would not give in. "I will not break my word. I will not turn against my friends."

"The Bostons are not your friends," Leschi told him. "They call you a spy.

They think you only pretend friendship."

Chief Seattle was deeply hurt.

"Your own people call you a traitor," the young chief went on, "because you will not fight for their rights."

Seattle looked around the council. He saw that this was true. His people believed he had turned against them.

Yet everything he had done had been for them! War would destroy them, he knew. Only through peace could there be any future for the Indians.

Slowly Chief Seattle rose. He stood tall and proud. "Whatever people call me," he thundered, "I will not go to war!"

10

War!

On the evening of January 25, a Suquamish scout returned to Ole-man-house. "Leschi plans to attack the Bostons tonight," he reported.

"I must warn the settlers," cried Dr. Maynard.

"No, doctor," said Chief Seattle. "Leschi would never let you return."

"Then I will go," said Catherine Maynard. "I will dress like an Indian woman."

"I will go with Mrs. Doctor," said Angeline. "Leschi will not bother two women."

"Do not go into the town," warned Seattle. "The fighting may break out any moment."

"We will warn the warship instead," Catherine answered. "The *Decatur* will protect the town."

Before midnight a canoe left the reservation. It carried the two women.

All night the chief and the doctor stood on the dark beach waiting. Just before dawn the canoe returned. Catherine and Angeline were safe. They had warned the *Decatur*.

A single great sound rolled across the bay from the town. "BOOM!"

The warship had fired its cannon. The battle had begun.

All day Chief Seattle stood on the beach in front of Ole-man-house. Frightened Indians milled around him. They begged to join Leschi. The chief neither saw nor heard them. He listened to the faint sounds of battle. He watched smoke rise above the town.

Chief Seattle felt as if his heart would break. His Indian friends were fighting his white friends. He had hoped this would never, never happen.

Had he been wrong? Seattle wondered. Was it impossible for white men and red to live in peace? Could they not learn from each other and help each other? Had Leschi been right, after all? Was war the only answer?

All through the long, long day Chief Seattle suffered. But he did not join Leschi. Not a single Indian crossed the sound from Ole-man-house reservation.

When the sun set behind the Olympic Mountains, the fighting stopped. Soon a scout returned from the town.

"There was much noise," he said. "Many guns were fired. But few were killed. Leschi has left. But he says he will return in one month and burn the settlement to the ground."

11

The Old Chief

Leschi did not attack the settlement again. Soldiers captured him instead.

Seattle tried to save the proud young chief. "Leschi rebelled against a bad treaty," he said. "Can a chief be blamed for trying to keep his people from starving?"

Governor Stevens refused to pardon Leschi. But he gave the Nisquallies a new reservation. They now had some good farmland.

Leschi said, "I have saved my people. This new reservation will enable them to live. I am content." Early in 1858, Leschi was hanged.

Chief Seattle lived at Ole-man-house reservation with his people. He knew they were not happy. Their old way of life was gone. They did not feel free, and the fishing and hunting were spoiled. They believed the Bostons had cheated them.

It took the United States Senate four years to approve the Indian treaties. Until then Chief Seattle's people had no money from the government. Dr. Maynard paid for their needs himself. He spent thousands of dollars.

Then Governor Stevens let Dr. Maynard go. He put another Indian agent in his place. Dr. Maynard moved back to Seattle. The government would not return the money he had spent.

The Indians missed the good doctor and his wife. They were more unhappy than ever.

For a long time Chief Seattle would not visit the town which bore his name. He was still hurt because the Bostons had not trusted him.

At last one day he paddled over to the town. David Denny saw him and called to him.

"Hello, Chief," he said. "It is good to see you again." How surprised Chief Seattle was at these friendly words! Then Arthur Denny called from his store, "Come in, Chief. I have some things to show you."

Later Seattle saw Henry Yesler. "Come down to the mill, Chief," said Mr. Yesler. "There have been many changes since you saw it last."

As Seattle walked to Dr. Maynard's house he was puzzled.

"What has happened?" he asked the doctor. "Yesterday the Bostons thought I was an enemy. Today they treat me as a friend."

"During the treaty troubles, the settlers were afraid of *all* Indians," Dr. Maynard told him. "Fear kept them from thinking straight. Now the trouble is over, and they realize that you have always been their friend."

Chief Seattle continued to live at Ole-man-house, but once in a while he visited the town.

When he was about 80, Chief Seattle became very sick. Dr. Maynard and other settlers visited him often, but no one could help him. On June 7, 1866, the old chief died.

Hundreds of people, both Indian and white, came to his funeral. They realized Seattle had been a great statesman.

Chief Seattle's son spoke. "My father was a great chief. He knew better what was good for Indians than we did ourselves. He kept us from war."

Dr. Maynard said, "Chief Seattle was the greatest friend of the whites on this side of America. We mourn his death."

As he spoke, the doctor seemed to hear Seattle's musical voice saying:

"There is no death, only a change of worlds."